# world writers
# Rick Riordan

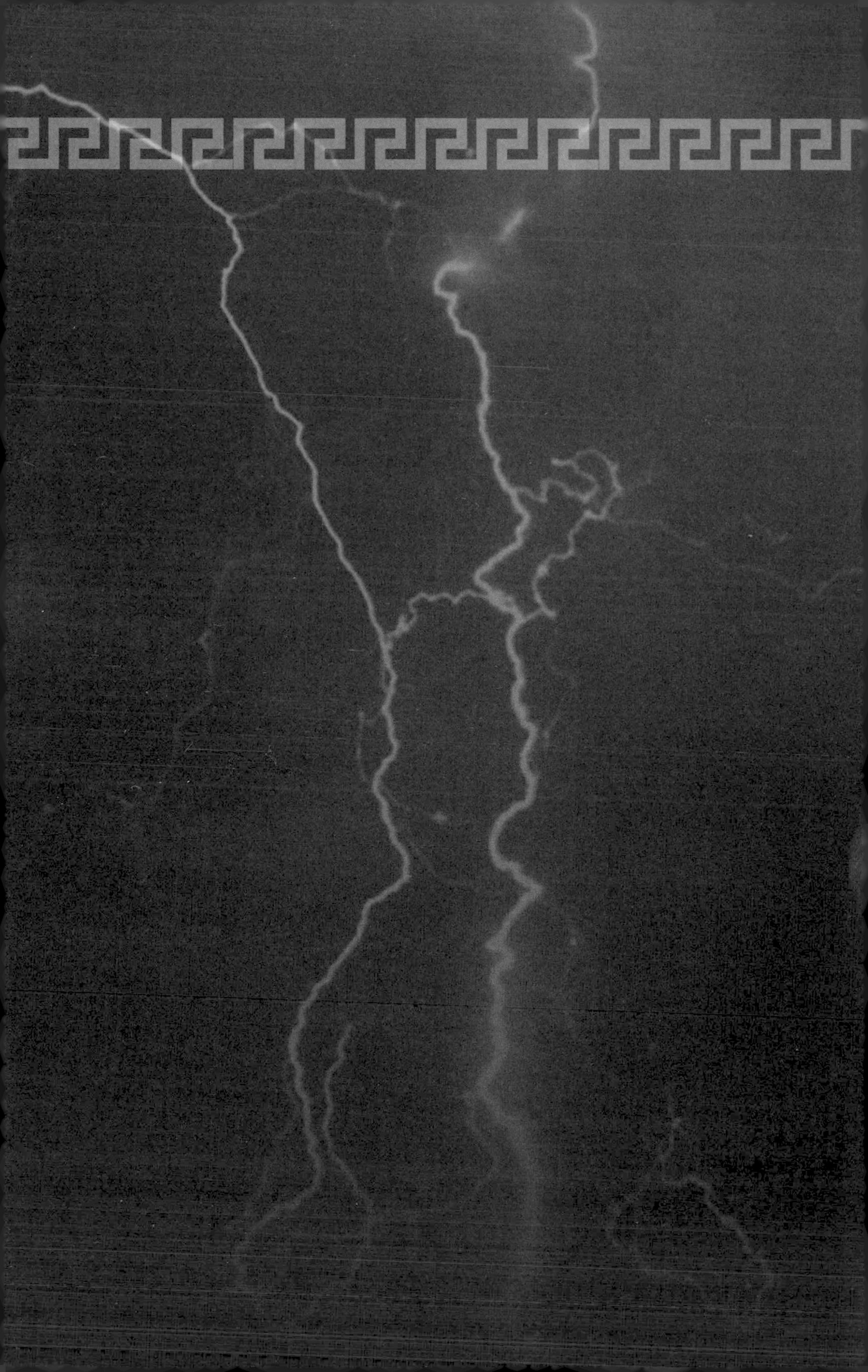

**world writers**
# Rick Riordan

## Barry Sparks

MORGAN
REYNOLDS
PUBLISHING

GREENSBORO, NORTH CAROLINA

For my grandchildren:
Colton, Michael, Ella, Maya and Miles

# World Writers Series

Rick Riordan

Library of Congress Cataloging-in-Publication Data

Sparks, Barry, 1949-
 Rick Riordan / by Barry Sparks.
   p. cm. --  (World writers)
 ISBN 978-1-59935-350-0 -- ISBN 978-1-59935-351-7 (e-book)
1.  Riordan,
Rick--Juvenile literature. 2.  Authors, American--20th
century--Biography--Juvenile literature.  I. Title.
 PS3568.I5866Z85 2012
 813'.54--dc23
 [B]

                                        2012018325

Printed in the United States of America
First Edition

Book cover and interior designed by:
Ed Morgan, navyblue design studio
Greensboro, NC

# TABLE OF CONTENTS

Rick Riordan signs copies of his books at the Book Expo America in New York on May 25, 2011.

# I CREATIVE INFLUENCES

Rick Riordan knew he wanted to be a writer when he was thirteen. His eighth-grade English teacher, Mrs. Pabst, had inspired him to write, telling him he might want to consider it as a career someday. Interested in science fiction and fantasy books, he wrote his first short story about angels. His teacher read the article and said, "Rick, this is great. Let's try to get it published."

She helped him submit the short story, "Appointment with an Archangel," to *Isaac Asimov's Science Fiction* magazine. Rick had visions of being a published writer. Every day, he excitedly ran to the mailbox to check for a letter from the editor. This went on for two months, which seemed like forever. Then a letter finally arrived. With his heart racing and his palms sweating, he tore open the envelope. Unfortunately, it was a rejection letter. The editor, however, offered some constructive criticism, writing that "angels aren't science fiction characters." He added, "You're really good for someone who's just 13, keep trying."

A Norse mythology image from the eighteenth century Icelandic manuscript *SÁM 66*, now in the care of the Árni Magnússon Institute in Iceland

Although he was dejected, his mother was proud of him. She proudly framed the rejection letter and hung it in the hallway where Rick would see it every day as a reminder of his effort and his dream. The rejection sucked a lot of enthusiasm out of Rick, and he didn't write anything for almost a year. But his dream was stronger than the rejection. Rick started writing again because he knew that one day he would be a published author.

Rick Riordan (pronounced RYE-or-dan) was born on June 5, 1964, in San Antonio, Texas. His parents, John and Lyn, were young Texas A & M college students.

It was a tumultuous time in America. President John F. Kennedy had been assassinated on November 22, 1963, in Dallas, Texas. Vice President Lyndon B. Johnson, a native of Texas, became president upon Kennedy's death. The day President Kennedy, who was very popular with young people, was assassinated was one of the saddest days in American history. The United States Congress was debating the Civil Rights Act which was passed later that summer. The Civil Rights Act of 1964 outlawed racial discrimination in public places such as restaurants, theaters, and hotels. It also required employers to provide equal employment opportunities. A relatively small number of American soldiers were fighting in South Vietnam. Under President Johnson, however, the war was beginning to escalate. It would be the subject of great debate among American leaders and the public. Eventually, the Vietnam War would fuel intense demonstrations and divide the public. Even the culture was changing. A British group of four long-haired musicians from Liverpool, England, called the Beatles were attracting record crowds of frenzied teens in the United States as they dominated the music charts. The Beatles—John, Paul, George, and Ringo—led the British music invasion which would influence teens in nearly every facet of life; from the clothes they wore to their hairstyles.

THE BEATLES IN 1964

It was not an easy time to be young parents, but John and Lyn Riordan were determined to give Rick as much love and stability as they could. Reflecting on his childhood, Riordan says he has great respect for the job his parents did. He is sure he could not have done as good of a job parenting as his parents did in their early twenties.

Both of Rick's parents were influential in his development. His father is creative and artistic. Growing up, Rick remembers his father as patient, caring, and humorous. When Rick was young, he clearly remembers crawling into bed between his parents and cuddling up to his dad, listening to his breathing until he fell asleep. His father had a strong and reassuring presence.

When Rick was a little older, his father became interested in pottery and learned how to use a pottery wheel to make ceramics. Rick tagged along with his father when he went to the art studio and to weekend art shows to sell his ceramics. Although Rick was never very good at using the pottery wheel, he enjoyed making clay sculptures, particularly dinosaurs. Rick remembers the time he made a dinosaur that came out of the kiln, an oven used to make ceramics, looking like it had melted. He described it as a dinosaur having a heart attack. His father said, "Well, bring it along. Maybe some sucker will buy it."

A POTTER MOLDS A POT ON A POTTERY WHEEL.

Sure enough, some customer saw the dinosaur, started laughing and reached in his pocket for money to buy it. As the transaction took place, Rick looked at his father and loudly exclaimed, "You were right, some sucker did buy it." His father turned red with embarrassment and signaled Rick not to say anymore until after the customer left.

Rick's father loved to read to him. He traces his lifelong love of mythology back to his father reading aloud stories from *Tales of the Western World* by Ruth Suddeth when he was in elementary school. The book features American Indian myths and tall tales from the pioneers. Rick still has a treasured, tattered copy of the book. Other books he remembers his father reading to him include the Dr. Seuss book *Hop on Pop* and P. D. Eastman's *Go Dogs Go.*

"The foundation of who I would become was laid in those early years, watching and learning from my father," says Rick. "Without a strong role model like him, I doubt I would've become a writer."

Rick's mother is also artistic and creative. He describes her as a Renaissance woman, someone who is an accomplished artist, musician, writer, and an extremely gifted teacher. She helped him tap into his creativity. Rick was not overly busy as a youngster, and he often told his mother he was bored. She would help him brainstorm about some possible ideas, but in the end, it was up to him to find something to do. "I'm convinced this turned me into a writer," he says. "I had to look inward for my own stories and my own fantasy worlds." His mother encouraged his writing, serving as his first reader, first editor, and first fan.

A self-described reluctant reader who would do anything to avoid reading in elementary school, Rick was more interested in imagining himself and his friends being attacked by Godzilla on the playground or thinking about what he was going to do after school. He did, however, enjoy his second-grade teacher, Mrs. Bostick, reading *Mrs. Pigglewiggle* and the *Boxcar Children* aloud to the class. She also got him interested in *Charlotte's Web* and *Trumpet of the Swan*, even though he professed to hate reading at the time. By sixth grade, he had begun reading some Greek mythology.

When Rick was twelve, his mother gave him a boxed set of J. R. R. Tolkien's trilogy Lord of the Rings, consisting of *Fellowship of the Ring*, *The Two Towers*, and *The Return of the Ring*. It proved to be a turning point in his life. "That boxed set is the most important Christmas gift I've ever received," he says. It captured his imagination and opened up an entire new world to him, spawning an interest in mythology, fantasy, and reading for pleasure. Lord of the Rings, published in 1954-1955, has been described as "a tale of enthralling adventures and mythical beings that touches upon some questions of philosophy and mortality. Heroic deeds, the uniting for the sake of a common cause, true love, the triumph of Good over Evil—all of these things can be found in this epic."

Other books Rick remembered reading around this time include a *Wizard of Earthsea* by Ursula Le Guin and *Stranger in a Strange Land* by Robert Heinlein. A little earlier, he enjoyed *Phantom Tollbooth* by Norton Juster. His favorite writers included Roald Dahl, E. B. White, and C. S. Lewis. He also delved deeper into Greek and Norse mythology tales.

AN 1858 STATUE OF IÐUNN, A GODDESS ASSOCIATED WITH APPLES AND YOUTH IN NORSE MYTHOLOGY, BY H. W. BISSEN

He loved the gods and goddesses because they were cool. He imagined his parents as Greek gods and himself as a hero. His other reading material included stacks of hand-me-down adventure and fantasy comic books and *Mad* magazines from his uncles.

It was around this time that Rick decided he wanted to be a teacher and a writer. His parents were both teachers, and he enjoyed listening to stories when he was a child. He recalls listening to adults spin tall tales of the Wild West around campfires. He paid attention to how the best storytellers held everyone's attention with the colorful and exaggerated tales. He remembers his grandfather, who was a colonel in the Air Force, telling him stories. Rick would sit on his lap, and his grandfather would open up his briefcase and pull out some pens and paper. He would draw pictures of paratroopers landing in a war zone, and they always found a secret cave to set up their home base. Rick thought having a secret cave was a cool thing. "Those times I spent with him instilled the love of storytelling in me," says Rick. "I still believe that telling stories can be one of the most powerful bonds two people can share."

Rick envisioned himself as a storyteller, but he had never met a writer and he wasn't sure how to become one. His teachers said, "Write what you know about." That was frustrating advice because

Rick didn't know much about anything, and what he did know was boring.

At Alamo Heights High School, Rick continued to write, focusing much of his effort on the school newspaper. The most memorable experience was when he and a friend published an underground edition of the school newspaper called the "Alamo Heights Lampoon." The edition poked fun at the school's hapless football team. Although school officials couldn't prove it, they believed Rick was behind the prank. In retaliation, members of the football team threw eggs at Rick's house.

He also began playing Dungeons and Dragons, a popular fantasy role-playing game, with his friends. The game is played with dice, miniature figures, and books that guide players. The game has been described as shared storytelling with social interactions. It involves a Dungeon Master and several players, each with a unique hero they build by choosing different powers. The Dungeon Master devises different encounters for each game. The heroes must work together to overcome situations and challenges. Other game characters include humans, dwarfs, clerics, rouges, fighters, warlocks, and warlords.

Given his parents' influence and his high school activities, it was only natural that Rick would explore music, arts, and writing after he graduated from high school in 1982. But he still had no idea where his interests would take him.

MINIATURE FIGURES USED IN
DUNGEONS AND DRAGONS

# II

# GETTING PUBLISHED

Beytt ſu er Hey Xi
gtir. Stend uppa
hōll t bytix bar a
um tries peß ex Eo
heitix Ñun ſniōlb e
og Handa ōllū Eyn
Leo XXXIII
Dæmi Sogu

Riordan attended North Texas State in Denton, where he temporarily set aside his dream to be a writer to focus most of his energy on music. He was going to major in music and hopefully become a rock star. With long hair and a mustache, Riordan was the lead singer in a folk rock band called Cheyenne. He looked like a combination of New Age singer Yanni and the Sgt. Peppers Club-era Beatle George Harrison. Riordan wrote some original songs, but he and his two high school friends mostly played songs by Bob Dylan, Neil Young, the Beatles, and the Rolling Stones. They played in nightclubs and restaurants throughout Texas. The band made enough money that Riordan didn't have to work any other job while attending college. While it was a fun experience, Riordan realized the band was probably not going to get a recording contract. And he wouldn't be a rock star. So he shifted gears to focus on other subjects. He transferred to the University of Texas at Austin. Before he graduated with a double degree in English and History, he published his first articles in the school's literary magazine.

THE GOAT HEIÐRÚN IN A NORSE MYTHOLOGY IMAGE FROM THE EIGHTEENTH CENTURY ICELANDIC MANUSCRIPT *NKS 1867 4TO*, NOW IN THE CARE OF THE DANISH ROYAL LIBRARY

The decade of the 1980s was a time of economic prosperity in the United States. A greater emphasis was put on making money, acquiring possessions, and looking out for yourself rather than others. It spawned the term the "me" generation. Many of the young people of this decade had a sense of entitlement. They felt they deserved great jobs, praise, and attention.

Helping others wasn't as important as it had been in the past. A survey of college freshman revealed that only 29 percent thought it was important to influence social values, and volunteerism was at an all-time low. Making money, and lots of it, was high on many people's list.

Although Riordan attended high school and college in the 1980s, he didn't succumb to the influences of the "me" generation. Having eliminated music as a career, Riordan was torn between journalism and teaching. While he enjoyed journalism, he realized it would probably require him to work weekends, holidays, and perhaps evenings. The salaries, particularly for entry-level positions, weren't appealing. It turned out that teaching was his fall-back position. It was something he enjoyed doing, and he was comfortable in the classroom. It would allow him to be a storyteller and get paid at the same time. He knew the teaching profession seldom led to a fancy lifestyle, but he was most interested in helping children in the classroom. When he became a teacher, he quickly realized that late-night performances with his band didn't fit in well with his teaching schedule. Going to bed late and getting up early to teach didn't mix. He gave up music and concentrated on teaching.

His first teaching job was at New Breunfels Middle School in Texas, one of the poorest school districts in San Antonio. Many of his students came from low-income families and participated in the free lunch program, which provided the only meal of the day for some of them. Most of his students' parents were on welfare, and only a few had a high school education. Despite their backgrounds, Riordan knew that these students had the same problems and needs as students from wealthier neighborhoods. His students needed self-confidence and their parents' attention, structure, and balance.

The middle school years are critical for students. It is a time of uncertainty and change—emotionally, intellectually, socially, and physically. Riordan was drawn to this age group because he remembered how formative those years were in his own life. It is a time when students either begin to find themselves or start to fall through the cracks. He wanted to make a difference. Riordan's goal as a teacher was to make it so much fun for students in his classroom that they wouldn't realize they were learning. He calls it subversive learning. Riordan's personality came out in the classroom. He was humorous, friendly, relaxed, creative, interesting, and entertaining. He often read stories aloud to his students and mesmerized them with his storytelling, which was a big part of his teaching style. Through storytelling, he learned to condense a story, make it relevant and funny while including plenty of action and adventure. Teaching was a gratifying profession.

Teaching, however, was just half of his dream. The other part was writing. He pursued that part of his dream by writing short stories in the evenings and on weekends. In 1988, he had several short stories published. "The Sheet Cave" and "Out on 1040" appeared in *Cactus Alley* and "A Small Silver Gun" was featured in *Family Circle Mary Clark Higgins Mystery*. His short stories also appeared in *Ellery Queen's Mystery Magazine*.

In 1990, he accepted a teaching position with Presidio Hill School, a prestigious, private school in San Francisco. The school's philosophy is learning by doing and students are encouraged to express themselves creatively. Working in such an environment was an exciting opportunity. Leaving Texas, however, was not easy for Rick and his wife, Becky, who had been his high school sweetheart. They would have to leave their relatives, friends, and way of life more than 1,700 miles behind.

After the Riordans were California residents for a while, something unexpected happened. Rick got homesick. He missed his parents, friends, the Texas culture, and even the unbearably hot and humid Texas weather. He started to realize how much he liked San Antonio. Failing to shake his homesickness, Riordan figured there might be a way he could channel that feeling. In high school and college, he was hooked on reading mysteries by authors such as Robert B. Parker, Raymond Chandler, and Dashiell Hammett. He found them intriguing and fascinating. On a lark, he decided to write a mystery, based in San Antonio.

"It was only after moving to San Francisco that I realized what a unique place San Antonio was," he says. "I needed distance to write effectively about my hometown." His teachers' advice to "write what you know about" started to make more sense. Riordan's mystery featured detective Tres (pronounced Trace) Navarre who leaves San Francisco to go home to San Antonio with the intention of marrying his high school sweetheart. Navarre isn't your ordinary detective. He's a Tai Chi master with a PhD in medieval literature. He has an enchilada-eating cat named Robert Johnson. Navarre pursues his private investigator's license after failing to find a job as a college professor.

SAN ANTONIO'S SKYLINE

Riordan never planned to write a mystery, but the plot and character of Tres Navarre popped into his head and wouldn't leave. Navarre makes decisions and goes down paths that Riordan didn't. He says Navarre is a "what if" version of himself. Navarre moved to San Francisco after witnessing the murder of his father, Sheriff Jackson Navarre. Now, after a decade, he returns home determined to solve his father's murder. Of course, digging up the past isn't popular with the townspeople, and he receives a rude reception for his efforts. Things don't go smoothly, but Navarre refuses to give up.

At the time, Americans were reading espionage thrillers by Ken Follet, Robert Ludlum, and Tom Clancy as well as legal thrillers by Scott Turow and John Grisham. Horror writer Stephen King and romance writer Danielle Steele were favorites, too. The most popular mystery writers were Tony Hillerman, whose books were set in Arizona and featured Navajo police officers Jim Chee and Joe Leaphorn, and Sue Grafton, who was working her way through the alphabet, title by title such as *A is for Arson*, *B is for Burglar*, with sleuth Kinsey Millhone. Juggling his responsibilities as a teacher, husband, and new father, his son Haley

NAVAJO
SANDSTONE

was born in 1995, Riordan started to write his novel, working in the early mornings, evenings, and on weekends. It was a grueling schedule, particularly since there was no guarantee of a financial payoff. He says it was important for him to write the story, whether it got published or not. He did have a suspicion, however, that it had a good chance of being published.

"It felt different than anything else I had ever done," he says, "and I really did have a compulsion to finish the manuscript in a way that nothing else had ever motivated me before." Riordan further says, "I knew, deep down, that this story would get published."

Friends asked Riordan how he found the time to write a novel while teaching full-time. Actually, he didn't find the time, he made the time. He maximized his time, limiting his recreational activities and not watching television. If a show was on television in the 1990s, he didn't see it. He jokes that it's not true, however, that teaching middle school students all day put him in the mood to write about murder.

Finishing the manuscript titled *Big Red Tequila* was only part of the challenge. Now, he had to find a publisher. This proved to be very frustrating. He submitted the four hundred-plus page manuscript to publisher after publisher, but always with the same result—rejection. One publisher said, "We love the story, but hate the characters." Another wrote, "We love the characters, but hate the story." One publisher candidly admitted, "We just don't like Texas." The rejections were crushing, but Riordan refused to give up. He took constructive criticism to heart and revised the manuscript multiple times. Finally, after thirteen rejections, a publisher accepted *Big Red Tequila*. Just shy of thirty, Riordan had accomplished his goal to be a published author.

*Big Red Tequila*, published as a paperback by Bantam, hit the bookstores in July 1997. Books written by first-time authors seldom generate much attention or publicity. But *Publisher's Weekly*, an influential publication about books, praised *Big Red Tequila* as "A stand out! What makes this a truly worthy debut is Riordan's voice . . . [and]unbeatable flair for detail." The *Portland Oregonian* described *Big Red Tequila* as, "Texas ambience served baking hot." It added, "This engaging private eye has an exciting career ahead of him." The *Chicago Tribune* wrote, "Riordan writes so well about the people and topography of his Texas hometown that he quickly marks the territory as his own." The *San Antonio Express-News* added, "Riordan's sense of place is excellent, his dialogue is properly gritty, but the plot could have used more pace."

THE ALAMO MISSION, THE SITE OF THE BATTLE OF THE
ALAMO, PART OF SAN ANTONIO'S RICH HISTORY

Publishing his first novel was the initial step on a
long journey to fame and fortune for Riordan, who
had no idea what the future would bring. One thing
it wouldn't bring, however, was overnight success.

# III PERCY JACKSON IS BORN

S hortly after the publication of *Big Red Te-quila*, Riordan was invited to a Waldenbooks in a Concord, California, shopping center for a book signing. He was scheduled to sign books for two hours. He had a table in front of the store, a stack of books, and unbridled enthusiasm. He proudly sat at the table, but no one approached him except to ask for directions to another store in the shopping center or where the self-help books were. He didn't sell any copies of his book. It was a long and disappointing afternoon. Unfortunately, that wasn't an isolated case. When he held his first book discussion in Oakland, only two people showed up. There were other disappointing book signings and discussions groups. "Today, I'm constantly amazed when I walk into a bookstore and there are actually people waiting for me," says Riordan.

Riordan received some much-needed uplifting news in 1998, when *Big Red Tequila* received the Anthony Award for Best Paperback and the Shamus Award for Best P. I. Paperback Original. The awards boosted Riordan's confidence and morale. After all, well-known mystery writers Jonathan Kellerman and Patricia Cornwell had won the Anthony Award in the same category and best-selling authors Walter Mosley and Dennis Lehane had captured a similar Shamus Award.

That same year, the first book by a relatively un-known British writer J. K. Rowling was released in the United States. *Harry Potter and The Sorcerer's Stone* featured Harry Potter, a young wizard. Rowling had submitted several sample chapters of her manuscript to the Christopher Little Agency, where a young as-sistant read them and recommended them to her boss. The agency offered Rowling a contract to represent her. Literary agents use their knowledge of the pub-lishing industry to interest a publisher in purchasing the writer's work and publishing it. Agents typically receive a percentage of the money the author receives. After twelve publishers passed on the opportunity, Bloomsbury Publishing, a small company, offered her $2,250 advance royalties to publish the book. First printing was only five hundred copies. The book was published in England in 1997 and became an instant hit, selling more than 100,000 copies in a few months

J. K.
ROWLING
IN 2010

and winning several prestigious awards. The book's success caught the attention of American publishers, and an auction was held for the United States rights. Arthur Levin of Scholastic Press won the bidding war with a $105,000 offer, the most ever paid for a children's book.

*Harry Potter and The Sorcerer's Stone* spent an unheard of fourteen weeks on the *New York Times* best seller list. It was a phenomenal feat for any book, much less a children's book. No other children's book had ever come close to matching Rowling's record. *Charlotte's Web* by E. B. White was most notable, spending three weeks on the *New York Times* best seller list in 1952. The magic and wizardry of Harry Potter captured the attention of boys and girls unlike any other book. The success of the Harry Potter series, seven books in all, would transform the world of young adult literature.

By now, Riordan was working on his next Tres Navarre mystery, *The Widower's Two-Step*. In the second book, Navarre is on the verge of gaining his private investigator's license. He's assigned to keep an eye on a musician who's suspected of stealing a demo tape of an up-and-coming country music star. Navarre has a serious lapse during his surveillance, taking his eyes off the suspect. By the time he returns his attention to the suspect, she's been shot. Despite being warned to leave the case to the cops, Navarre persists and lands in the middle of a war in the music industry. A review in the *San Antonio Express-News* stated, "Riordan shows measurable progress as an author in this, his second novel . . . Riordan's writing, plotting and characterizations are stronger than in *Big Red Tequila*."

Riordan's profile as an author spiked when the Mystery Writers of America selected *The Widower's Two-Step* to receive an Edgar Award for Best Paperback Original. An Edgar Award is widely acknowledged as the most prestigious award in the genre.

WRITER WALTER MOSLEY, (*LEFT*), S. J. ROZAN, (*CENTER*), AND RICK RIORDAN AT THE EDGAR AWARDS IN NEW YORK CITY IN 2003

With his first two novels, Riordan had earned mystery genre's three most prestigious awards—The Edgar, the Anthony, and the Shamus. It was an amazing accomplishment. Despite his success, Riordan wasn't tempted to give up his teaching job to become a full-time writer. Only a handful of full-time writers can make a living. Teaching offered a number of advantages. He had a steady income, benefits, and security. And, with a wife and child, these were important. It was too scary to gamble on the uncertainty of writing full-time. Plus, he enjoyed teaching.

After the publication of *The Widower's Two-Step*, the Riordans decided to move back to San Antonio.

They had been returning to San Antonio twice a year to visit relatives, friends, and for Riordan to conduct research for his Tres Navarre series. He figured if he was going to keep the series going, he needed to live in San Antonio. Moving back home would also give his son more time with his grandparents. Riordan took a teaching position at Saint Mary's Hall, a prestigious private school founded in 1879. It boasts some of the most dedicated, creative, and dynamic teachers and a reputation for academic excellence. Riordan was a perfect match with the school.

In his third Tres Navarre novel, *The Last King of Texas*, Navarre is hired to replace a University of Texas at San Antonio professor who was shot and killed after receiving threatening letters. Navarre can't resist investigating the murder, and soon he's uncovering family secrets about the carnival business that served as a cover-up for running drugs. *The Last King of Texas* was Riordan's first hardback book, reflecting a vote of confidence from his publisher. It was also a featured alternate for the Mystery Guild book club. Reviewers praised the book. Oline Gogdill, a columnist for the *Fort Lauderdale Sun-Sentinel* wrote, "It's appropriate that *The Last King of Texas* is paced like a well-oiled carnival ride:

The story has barely begun before author Riordan provides twists, turns and a couple of loop-the-loops before the thrill ride really picks up speed . . . . And like a good carnival ride, just when you think all the surprises have been played out, Riordan pulls out that last little snap, that surprise curve just so you don't forget what a satisfying ride this has been."

Despite the praise, there were no major awards for *The Last King of Texas*. Riordan's books were steady, dependable sellers, but they weren't capturing a national audience. He was well-known in Texas and parts of the South, but not in places like Chicago and Boston. He was settling into becoming a mid-list author, one who has a loyal fan base but whose sales of individual books don't reach six figures. His books weren't heavily marketed. But Riordan knew that only a handful of authors attract national attention, make the best seller lists, and become wealthy. He was content teaching middle school students and writing the Tres Navarre novels, which his students sometimes read. They often pleaded with him to let them write book reports about the novels. Riordan told the students the books weren't appropriate for middle school, and there were plenty of other books they could review. That didn't keep his students from reading the Tres Navarre books.

With each book, Riordan was honing his writing skills. He was learning more about plotting, pacing, and developing characters. In the beginning, he used a flowchart program called "Inspiration" to make brainstorming maps. He would print out massive sheets and pin them to a wall. It was very helpful for him to visualize the flow of the novel. Every square represented a chapter, and he would move them around as needed. He learned to internalize the process, making the visuals unnecessary. Now, he writes a short outline with a paragraph for each chapter. He writes a quick draft, which generally follows the outline, and then spends a lot of time revising.

In June 2001, *The Devil Went Down to Austin* was published. Tres's older brother, Garrett, a hippie and Jimmy Buffet fan who lost both of his legs in a train accident, gets into trouble, and Tres wants to clear his brother's name. As usual, he sticks his nose where some people don't think it belongs.

The following year, Riordan published his first novel, *Cold Springs*, that didn't feature Tres Navarre. He didn't plan to take a break from the Navarre series, but an idea, based on his personal experience as a teacher, grabbed him and wouldn't let go. While teaching in San Francisco, an eighth-grade girl with emotional problems ran away from home and was returned by police. She disappeared from school again weeks later. This time, however, her mother had put the girl in a wilderness program at the suggestion of a counselor. The girl was taken from her home in the middle of the night by a program escort and taken to a plane in her pajamas. She returned to school six weeks later with almost no personality. This disturbed Riordan. He used the book to write about wilderness programs and the effect they have on students. Writing *Cold Springs* was a huge growth experience for Riordan. It was darker than his other novels, and it was written from multiple perspectives. Additionally, it was set in two different places at once. The American Library Association placed the book on its Top 10 suspense novels list.

Riordan reached a pinnacle in his teaching career in 2002 when he received a Master Teacher Award from Saint Mary's Hall. The award included $10,000.

Riordan was one of four educators to win the award in its first year. More than one hundred teachers were nominated. A Saint Mary's Hall patron donated $1 million in 2001 to fund four Master Teacher Awards each year. When Riordan's name was announced as a recipient of the award, his students cheered enthusiastically. "I should probably come up with something brilliant to say, but I'm stunned," he said. "I wasn't expecting this; I don't know that I did anything special. I was just enjoying myself in the classroom."

Around this time, Riordan's eight-year-old son, Haley, was struggling in school. Recently diagnosed with learning disabilities, he hated school. He didn't like to read or do homework assignments. Riordan, who had earned a reputation as a riveting storyteller in the classroom, was desperate to find books Haley would like to read. He tried all different types of books, from science fiction to detective stories. Nothing worked. The concerned father discovered, however, that Haley was interested in Greek mythology, a subject he taught to his middle school students. Riordan began telling Greek mythology tales to Haley at bedtime. He regaled his son with the stories of Jason and the Argonauts, Hercules, Medusa, and many others.

The bedtime tales continued for many nights until Riordan had exhausted all the Greek myths he knew. Enthralled with the stories, Haley begged his father to tell him more. There aren't any more, his father sadly informed him. "Why can't you just make some up?" Haley asked.

Like any father, Riordan didn't want to disappoint his son, who now looked forward to the nightly bedtime stories. He thought about a creative writing assignment he used with his sixth graders. He asked the students to create their own demigod, the son or daughter of any god and mortal they wanted. And, they had to write about a Greek-style quest for that hero.

Using this premise, Riordan made up the story about Perseus (Percy) Jackson, a demigod who is the son of the Greek god Poseidon and a mortal woman. Jackson's quest was to recover Zeus's lightning bolt which had been stolen and return it to him to prevent a war of the gods. The twelve-year-old Jackson travels across the United States in modern times on the often-dangerous quest. Riordan told the story in three nights.

At its conclusion, the spellbound Haley told his father to write the story of Percy Jackson down as a book. Riordan thought, "No one will be interested in this story; it's a personal story just for you." But, Haley persisted. So Riordan began writing the adventures of Percy Jackson. That's how one of the most popular characters of all-time in young adult literature was created. The tale would become the best-selling book *The Lightning Thief.*

# IV   THE LIGHTNING THIEF

As if Riordan's life wasn't busy or hectic enough writing a Tres Navarre novel a year and teaching full-time, now he was squeezing another book into his crammed schedule. When he was writing *The Lightning Thief,* he was also working on *Southtown,* his fourth Tres Navarre novel. It was challenging, but Riordan firmly believes that when you really want to do something, you'll find the time. At first, he would write *Southtown* one week and *The Lightning Thief* the next. Then he switched to working on one book in the morning and the other book after school and in the evenings. He was writing about three or four hours a day. Riordan was confident he could write a young adult fantasy book. After all, he had already written five mystery novels. He understood how to tell an entertaining story and how to create scenes and dialog. He tested plots, dialogue, and jokes on his Saint Mary's Hall students.

Riordan believes working on the Percy Jackson book made his Tres Navarre book better.

"Kids are a much tougher audience than adults," he says. "They won't sit through a bunch of extraneous information and description. The writer has to get to the point quickly and hold the reader's interest."

Riordan always imagined himself reading his own book aloud to his sixth graders in fifth period, right after lunch. That's the most difficult time to keep their attention. If his book could keep the entire class's attention, not just the A students, but also the C students, he knew he had a winner on his hands. While writing *The Lightning Thief*, Riordan paid particular attention to the storyline, making sure he kept the tension high and never letting the action lag. He believes children as well as adults are looking for the same thing in a book—characters who are sympathetic, humor, a plot that pulls them through the book, and a situation they can relate to. He spent about a year writing the Percy Jackson book. He didn't tell anyone about it except his immediate family. He found it surprisingly easy to write. He enjoyed it because the story was so much fun and so different from his mystery novels.

Even though he felt confident about the Percy Jackson manuscript, he wasn't sure how it would be received or if he could get it published. He expected it to be rejected. After all, his first Tres Navarre novel had been rejected thirteen times. He submitted it to several agents under the pseudonym Ransome Reese (the name of one of his distant relatives) because he wanted the book to succeed or fail on its own merits. He purposely did not submit it to the publisher of his Tres Navarre novels. Riordan sent the first draft of *The Lightning Thief* to Nancy Galt, an independent literary agent for children's books based in South Orange, NJ. It took her nearly six weeks to get a chance to read it. When she did, she thought it was fabulous. She sent the book out to several publishers, and it generated a high level of interest, totally surprising Riordan. Some of the publishers, however, were reluctant to bid on the book because Riordan had used a pseudonym. He quickly agreed to use his real name, and an intense bidding competition began. Miramax, a division of Disney, was the high bidder. Miramax offered Riordan a three-book contract and a sizable advance, which allowed Riordan to quit his teaching job at Saint Mary's Hall. Although Riordan didn't disclose the amount of the advance, he said, "This is a whole different world for me. It's certainly head and shoulders above what I receive for my adult fiction."

Brenda Bowen, vice president and editor in chief of Hyperion Books for Children, a division of Disney, said, "It's a book that combines an ordinary boy (well, not so ordinary), a cross-country chase, a Greyhound bus and Greek gods. Who wouldn't be interested?" She also praised Riordan for his ability to combine disparate elements, a trick she says every author wishes he or she could pull off, but very few can. The book was projected as a back-to-school novel for middle school students. It would be one of the publisher's major titles and supported with a major promotional campaign.

Quitting teaching after fifteen years wasn't an easy decision for Riordan. He enjoyed being in the classroom, working closely with students, and making a difference in their lives. But it ended up just being a question of time. He didn't think he could do justice to his family, students, or his writing by continuing to teach full-time and write. Riordan believes you can take the teacher out of the classroom, but not the classroom out of the teacher. He still considers himself a teacher. Now, however, instead of having twenty or thirty students in a class, he has millions of students. His goal, like it was in the classroom, is to turn children into readers and get them to learn without them realizing it. "I want to inspire them to learn more, to become life long readers and learners, and you can only do that by making the subject matter engaging."

Before *The Lightning Thief* would be published, however, Riordan's fourth Tres Navarre novel, *Southtown*, would hit the bookstores. In the book, Navarre gets caught in the middle of an escaped mass murderer's desire for revenge.

*The Lightning Thief* was published on July 28, 2005, with a modest first printing of 35,000 copies. Riordan was filled with excitement and anxiety. After writing for ten years, he had a gut feeling this was his chance to break through as an author. Yet, it looked like the chance might slip away. When he and his family visited the Oakland-San Francisco area that summer, he was looking for signs *The Lightning Thief* was generating interest. But, he was disappointed. Riordan and his family visited a number of bookstores with the intention of signing copies of *The Lightning Thief.* The stores, however, didn't have any copies of the newly released book in stock. Riordan held a book signing at one store, and the crowd was sparse. Disappointed, Riordan went back to the hotel and curled up in a fetal position. "That's it," he thought. "Nobody likes Percy Jackson. It's hopeless."

Riordan was determined to do everything he could to increase the sales of the book. He toured throughout the country for the next six months, visiting countless schools and bookstores. *The Lightning Thief* received a big boost when it made the Texas Library Association's Bluebonnet list of highly recommended books. Then it started showing up on other state lists, and word began to spread. Librarians, particularly those in Texas, were the first champions of the book. They forged a grassroots effort to get *The Lightning Thief* into the hands of their students. Additionally, booksellers and teachers touted the book. Perhaps most importantly, students were enthusiastic about it and shared their enjoyment of the book with their peers. Librarians found it difficult to keep the book on the shelves, and there were long reserved lists.

*The Lightning Thief* appeals to preteens and teens for many reasons. "Who wouldn't want to be the son or daughter of a Greek god," asks Riordan, who says fantasy and mythology have always been popular with kids. "We have a desire to believe in heroes, and that regular people have special powers and do extraordinary things." Riordan believes Greek mythology is a phase in kids' reading, appealing to just the age he was trying to reach, ages eight to twelve. "There's so much to spark the imagination," he says. "Mystery and monsters and villains and heroes and romance, everything you could want." And, the stories are timeless. Riordan says while we tend to think of divorce and complicated families as a modern invention, we only have to read Greek myths to see broken homes, widows, divorce, stepchildren, and children trying to get along with their parents.

> "WHO WOULDN'T WANT TO BE THE SON OR DAUGHTER OF A GREEK GOD?"
> – RICK RIORDAN

When Riordan speaks to school groups he often asks students what Greek god they would like for a parent. His favorite answer was from a girl in Texas who shouted out "Batman." Of course, Batman is a comic book character, not a Greek god. But Riordan says the idea of Batman being a Greek god isn't far off. "It's the same idea at work: creating a superhuman version of humanity so that we can explore our problems, strengths and weaknesses. If the novel puts life under the microscope, mythology blows it up billboard size."

Students relate to Percy Jackson, who has to deal with many of the same issues they do—everyday problems at school, family relationships, and feeling like you don't belong. He's adventuresome and courageous but not perfect. He's insecure and flawed. He has been kicked out of every school he's ever attended, and he's never earned a grade higher than C-plus. He's an underdog turned hero.

The book also includes heavy doses of humor, something middle school students love. Riordan, who injects humor into all of his books, realizes how critical it is. No matter how dire the situation is, he believes there's always room for humor. Riordan says middle school is "about being irreverent, it's about questions, it's about not taking everything seriously and looking at everything with kind of a sarcastic eye."

Middle schoolers relate to the idea of demigods who are half-god and half-man and who don't fit in either world. Demigods have huge challenges they must overcome. Riordan says this is an appropriate metaphor for being a middle schooler because they're not kids and they're not adults. They don't feel like they fit in. "They're stuck in the middle like a demigod," says Riordan. "Every challenge feels like a Herculean challenge, so they can relate to the Greek myth hero."

*The Lightning Thief* was well received. Polly Shulman wrote in the *New York Times*, "*The Lightning Thief* is perfectly paced, with electrifying moments chasing each

A 1650 STATUE DEPICTING THE DEMIGOD HERCULES

other like heartbeats, and mysteries opening out in sequence. The action never feels gratuitous; it draws its depth from myths at its source."

Jennifer Besser, Riordan's editor at Hyperion Books, wrote that reading *The Lightning Thief* gives you a feel for what kind of teacher Riordan was during his fifteen years in the classroom.

That same magic is present in *The Lightning Thief*. "He's the teacher you never forget, the one who makes the subject come alive and gets you truly excited to be in his class every day—and that's exactly what he's done in his writing," she commented.

*Mission Road*, Riordan's fifth Tres Navarre novel, was released the same month as *The Lightning Thief*. It marked a rare occurrence of an author having two books published in the same month. In *Mission Road*, Navarre tries to prove an old friend is innocent after being charged with homicide.

In 2006, *The Lightning Thief* won the Red House Children's Award, the only national children's book award voted for entirely by children. It gave *The Lightning Thief* a major boost, producing national publicity. It was also tremendously rewarding to Riordan, who considers it the best kind of award since it came directly from readers. Too often, he says, children are left out of the equation when it comes to book awards. As a middle school teacher,

Riordan knows firsthand that many of the award-winning children's books appeal to adults and teachers, but not children.

These books are often on required reading lists. But they bore children, often turning them off to reading. Riordan points to a statistic that says 58 percent of adults never read another book after high school. He blames part of it on the books students are required to read in middle school and high school. Riordan believes any book that makes a child want to read is a five-star book, and there's no award needed. The ultimate reward is when he receives an e-mail from a child saying, "Your book was the first book I ever enjoyed," or "Your book makes me want to write my own stories." That kind of feedback reminds Riordan why he became a writer in the first place.

While the momentum for Percy Jackson and *The Lightning Thief* was slowly building, Riordan was busy at work on the second book of the series, *Sea of Monsters*. He was, however, still full of doubt about whether the series would succeed.

# A Legion of Fans Grows

Riordan felt pressure writing *Sea of Monsters*. He had to recreate the magic of *The Lightning Thief*, and he knew it would be inevitably compared to his first book. That's why he believes the second book of a series is always the most difficult to write.

*Sea of Monsters* was released in May 2006. The sequel has Percy and his friends Annabeth and Tyson, a six-foot-three, mentally challenged homeless kid, trying to rescue Grover, their satyr friend. A cyclops has taken Grover prisoner on an island somewhere in the Sea of Monsters, which is known today as the Bermuda Triangle. Camp Half Blood, home of the demigods, is also at risk. The tree that protects the camp has been poisoned, making an attack by the Titans likely. Percy and friends must bring the Golden Fleece back to Camp Half Blood to heal the poisoned tree.

A Norse mythology image from *NKS 1867 4to*

Although *Publisher's Weekly* gave the book a starred review and noted "Riordan crafts a sequel stronger than his compelling debut," Riordan refused to rest on his laurels, questioning whether or not he had been right thinking the series would connect with kids. He talked to the publisher and his agent about what he could do to boost sales. Riordan continued to tirelessly visit countless schools and bookstores across the country. Word-of-mouth continued to be the best advertising. Once the Scholastic Book Club video featured *Sea of Monsters*, the momentum picked up. Soon, the book was making state reading lists. The book sold more than 100,000 copies in paperback and was named a *Child Magazine* Best Book for Children in 2006. It was nominated for the 2006 *Book Sense* Top 10 Summer Pick and later for the 2009 Mark Twain Award.

After the release of *Sea of Monsters*, Topher Bradfield, children's outreach coordinator for Book-People in Austin, came up with the idea of hosting a real Camp Half Blood. The week-long day camp featured lessons in mythology, swordplay, Greek dance, and drumming. The first camp attracted fifty-five children and by 2009, Camp Half Blood was attracting more than three hundred kids from around the world.

Percy was developing a legion of fans fascinated by demigods, mythology, and adventure. He became a role model for many young readers who never had one before. Percy is an unusual hero because he is dyslexic and has Attention Deficit Hyperactivity Disorder (ADHD). In developing the character, Riordan wanted to have someone with whom his son, Haley, who is dyslexic and ADHD, could relate.

Children with ADHD have difficulty paying attention, are hyperactive, or behave impulsively, often not considering the result of their actions. More boys than girls are diagnosed with ADHD. It affects 3 to 5 percent of school-aged children.

Dyslexia is characterized by difficulties with word recognition, poor spelling, and decoding abilities. Children with dyslexia have trouble reading, spelling, writing, and comprehending what they read.

ADHD IS ONE OF THE MOST COMMON NEUROBEHAVIORAL DISORDERS OF CHILDHOOD. IT IS NOT CLEAR WHAT CAUSES IT.

STUDENTS GET A CHANCE TO TOUR A MOBILE
CLASSROOM THAT SCREENS FOR DYSLEXIA AND READING
COMPLICATIONS AT THE ALFRED I. DUPONT HOSPITAL
FOR CHILDREN IN WILMINGTON, DELAWARE.

As a result of being dyslexic and ADHD, Haley
had many problems in school. When he was five
years old, he would hide under a table and cry when
it came time to study. Sometimes, he wanted to run
from his classroom. He was full of pent-up energy
and often blurted out during other people's conver-
sations. He constantly tried to avoid school work
with diversionary tactics such as sharpening his pen-
cil over and over, finding a household chore to do,
or feigning interest in any other topic.

Children with dyslexia and/or ADHD often have
low self-esteem. Riordan, however, wanted to show

his son and the rest of the world that there's no reason to be ashamed of dyslexia and ADHD. Through his own research, Riordan knew most kids with dyslexia or ADHD grow up to be successful adults. In fact, he discovered that a disproportionate number of millionaires are dyslexic. And, people with ADHD are valuable in the workplace because they focus intently on topics that interest them. Kids with learning differences become good out-of-the-box thinkers because they have to learn different ways to solve problems. Their biggest challenge is getting through school.

Making Percy Jackson dyslexic and ADHD was Riordan's way of honoring the potential of these kids. Riordan proposed the idea that exhibiting these conditions was a clear indication that you were special—perhaps even a demigod. Here's how he explains it: "Dyslexia . . . is simply the natural confusion that arises when you're hard-wired to read ancient Greek but forced to read English. ADHD is a side effect of the need to constantly survey your surroundings for monsters eager to destroy children who are part-mortal, part-god."

Children and parents bombarded Riordan with questions about Percy Jackson. One of the first letters he received was from a girl who wrote, "I used to feel like dyslexia was a curse. Now, I wear it as a badge of honor. I'm a demigod." Another letter came from a mother who said she was told her dyslexic daughter would never read a book. Then she started reading Percy Jackson, and her mother found her with a flashlight, under the covers, trying to finish the last book by herself. Riordan received many similar letters about children with ADHD. He couldn't imagine any better feedback.

Closer to home, Riordan saw the difference Percy Jackson made with Haley, who is now interested in reading and writing. Before his junior year in high school, he wrote a six hundred-page novel and planned to get it published before high school graduation. Haley's message to others with ADHD, dyslexia, or Asperger's syndrome, a developmental disorder that affects one's ability to socialize and communicate with others, is it's not a negative, but rather a positive. "You can do so much in your life that other people can't do," he stresses.

Riordan says kids with learning disabilities are modern versions of what it's like to be a hero. "You don't have to have magic powers to be a hero. It's about bravery and not listening when someone says you can't do something. A lot of kids have learning problems. It doesn't mean they aren't bright and creative and able to succeed."

People sometimes ask Riordan if he got the idea of Percy Jackson from Harry Potter. Riordan's reply to the question is "No—I got it from Hercules, 3,000 years earlier" than Harry Potter. There are, of course, several similarities between Percy Jackson and Harry Potter. They attend boarding schools for children with special powers, have a female sidekick, a male best friend, and special worlds. Riordan says Percy Jackson is similar to Harry Potter, not because he tried to model Percy after Harry, but because they are of the same archetype.

Riordan explains that J. K. Rowling bases much of the Harry Potter series on Greek mythology: the idea of magic being in the world; of great forces that are not seen; a young protagonist who is outcast but then finds out he actually has a great destiny; he has great abilities but needs to go to a trainer to get them recognized; he has to realize his destiny by taking on a quest and accomplishing a great task. "I've just described Harry Potter. But I've also just described Hercules, Percy Jackson, Perseus and Theseus," he says.

PERSEUS WITH THE HEAD OF MEDUSA BY ANTONIO CANOVA IN 1801

Riordan, however, is the first to admit Rowling had an influence. He recognized how she appealed to readers by combining humor, action, mystery, adventure, and character. As a teacher, he witnessed the powerful effect Rowling had on young readers. The Harry Potter series turned students onto reading in an unprecedented fashion. As a classroom teacher, Riordan had never seen anything like it. Almost over night, reading became cool. He recalled that students would read a Harry Potter book thirteen or fourteen times. When he asked why they didn't try another author or book, they replied, "Because there's nothing else this good."

Riordan was busy working on his third book in the series to keep the momentum building. All of his personal appearances and the enthusiasm of librarians and students were beginning to pay off. In March 2007, Riordan and his family were standing in line at a car rental agency in Las Vegas when he received a phone call from his publicist in New York City. She told him *The Lightning Thief* would be number six on the *New York Times* paperback best sellers list on Sunday, March 25. It was incredible news, almost two years after *The Lightning Thief* made its debut. Although Riordan had dreamed about making the *New York Times* best seller list, he never thought it would really happen. *The Lightning Thief* had received a recent boost from being featured on Al Roker's Book Club on the *Today Show*.

By this time, author J. K. Rowling had announced that the seventh book in her series, *Harry Potter and the Deathly Hallows*, would be the final one. The book was released on July 21 and sold an incredible 15 million copies in the first twenty-four hours. That's more than 10,400 books a minute. It set a record for the fastest-selling book of all-time, breaking the previous mark of 9 million by *Harry Potter and the Half-Blood Prince*. It marked the end of an era in which Harry Potter dominated the best seller lists, captured the imagination of millions, and revolutionized children's literature.

Of course, Riordan had followed the series closely, calling it wonderful. He was sorry to see it end. But, at the same time, he hoped Rowling stuck to her decision to end the series at seven books. Nothing should go on forever. And, it's best if a series ends on a satisfying note. He acknowledged, however, that some fans would never tire of Harry Potter and would eagerly buy Harry Potter number twenty-eight.

The big question was: What impact would the end of the Harry Potter series have on the Percy Jackson series? Would Percy prove to be a worthy successor to Harry, the most popular boy in the world?

Children eagerly wait in line for *Harry Potter and the Deathly Hallows* on June 21, 2007, the day the book was released.

# Myths, Mystery, and a Unique Series

The Percy Jackson craze was most evident in libraries. Librarians had to start hiding their read aloud copies because students kept taking them off their desks. Students suddenly started checking out books from the mythology section. Some of the books hadn't been checked out in years and had actually collected dust. But Riordan had fueled a renewed interest in mythology. Riordan's favorite retelling of the Greek myths is Bernard Evslin's *Heroes, Gods and Monsters of the Greek Myths*. It's the book that first got Riordan interested in mythology. Riordan also recommends the following books based on mythology: *The Pig Scrolls* by Paul Shipton, *The Shadow Thieves* by Anne Ursu, and *The Sea of Trolls* by Nancy Farmer.

A NORSE MYTHOLOGY IMAGE FROM *SÁM 66*

In the third Percy Jackson book, *The Titan's Curse*, Percy and his friends are on a quest to rescue his friend Annabeth and Artemis, a Greek goddess, who have been kidnapped. Percy and his friends have only a week to rescue the pair. Artemis was hunting down a powerful monster, which could destroy Olympus. She may be the only one who knows how to track him. Percy must battle the evil titan Kronos to succeed.

*Kirkus Review* wrote, "High-powered action sequences, humorous transposition of Olympian legends to the modern day and direct, unassuming narration remain a big draw for fans of the series, who will enjoy imagining themselves in the young heroes' dilemmas."

*The Titan's Curse* became a number one *New York Times* best seller. By this time, the *New York Times* had created a separate best seller list specifically for children's books. The move was made because author J. K. Rowling's Harry Potter books dominated the traditional list.

During the 2007-2008 school year, Riordan made seventy appearances to schools and bookstores, promoting *The Titan's Curse*. He spent a week visiting schools in the United Kingdom. He appeared on the *Today Show* for Al Roker's Book Club for Kids. Students were proclaiming it the best book in the series. By the end of April 2008, Percy Jackson books

RIORDAN AT THE 2007 TEXAS BOOK FESTIVAL
IN AUSTIN, TEXAS

had been on the *New York Times* children's best seller list for fifty-two consecutive weeks.

Four months later, the final Tres Navarre novel, *Rebel Island*, was released. Navarre and his wife, Maia Lee, who is eight months pregnant, take a belated honeymoon, arranged by his brother, Garrett, to Rebel Island. Tres and Garrett vacationed there as children. A hurricane and a murder of a U.S. Marshal set the stage for an intriguing tale that mixes the past and the present.

Although the Tres Navarre novels had been well received and praised, they were not nearly as successful as the Percy Jackson books. While *Rebel Island* sold 10,000 copies in hardcover and paperback, *Sea of Monsters* sold 1 million copies. The demands on Riordan's time made it difficult to continue the Tres Navarre series. While he has devoted all of his time to being a children's author since *Rebel Island* was published, he would never rule out writing for adults again.

Riordan's popularity reached a new plateau with the publication of *Battle of the Labyrinth*, which had a first printing of 1 million copies. Percy Jackson fans couldn't wait for his next adventure. First-week sales of *Battle of the Labyrinth* surpassed sales of *The Titan's Curse* in its first three months. In the adventure, Percy and his friends try to prevent Luke, another demigod, from resurrecting the Titan lord Kronos, whose goal is to overthrow the gods. When the heroes learn that Luke can breach Camp Half-Blood security through an exit in Daedaleus's Labyrinth,

A LABYRINTH

they enter the maze in search of the inventor and a way to stop the invasion.

During his public appearances, students often ask Riordan what it takes to become a writer. He has three tips for them: Read a lot. Write a little bit every day since writing is like a sport, the more you practice the better you become. And, don't get discouraged. Rejection is part of being a writer. No one is successful every time, and you must be willing to stick with it.

To be a writer, it's not enough to love the idea of writing or dream about being published. It's a lot of hard work. You must have a story you want to tell that is so compelling you simply have to write it. You have to forget about your goal of being published.

When adults tell Riordan they are considering quitting their job to become a writer, he cautions them to give it some thought. After all, he wrote for ten years and published six novels before being able to quit his full-time job. Most people can't make enough money writing to do it full time. Others say they will write a book when they have time or when they retire. He says the only way to accomplish it is to make time. He tells people not to wait because they will always be too busy. "No book has ever been written because the author had spare time to write it," he said.

What inspires Riordan as a writer? It's simple—deadlines and fan mail. Adhering to deadlines is how he was able to write the Tres Navarre novels while teaching. Riordan loves hearing from people who enjoy his books. That makes him want to write the next book even more and make it as good as possible.

When he was writing and teaching, Riordan wrote about three or four hours a day. When he quit teaching, he figured he would be able to write twice as long. But that hasn't been the case. He still writes about three or four hours a day. He doesn't have a set routine; every day is different. Some days he'll write in fifteen-minute spurts for a few hours, and other days he may write intensely from 8 a.m. to 8 p.m.

Riordan writes the first draft of a book in about two months and then spends the rest of the year revising it. He typically does four comprehensive revisions before he sits down to read it to his two sons, Haley and Patrick, who he considers valuable in-house critics and editors. Reading the story to them is very helpful in his revision process. He watches their expressions to see if the book is moving too slow or the jokes aren't as funny as he thought they were. If they beg him not to stop and read another chapter, he knows the story's working. Much of Riordan's success is built on knowing his audience.

As a teacher, he constantly stressed to his writing students the importance of having a sense of the audience.

The first Percy Jackson book hadn't yet taken off when Scholastic Books approached Riordan about a unique concept involving online gaming, trading cards, books, and $100,000 in prize money. Scholastic wanted to explore how publishing was going to shift as technology changes and how stories could be told differently. The planned ten-book series, The 39 Clues, would center around historical figures and the quest to find clues that would unlock the secret of ultimate power. Each book would reveal one clue, and readers would have to go online to discover the other thirty-eight. Children would be encouraged to decode secret messages contained in the books. Scholastic planned to feature trading cards sold in packs, and they would be included inside each book. The cards would contain codes which would lead to more clues when children typed them into The 39 Clues gaming Web site. Scholastic's team of editors developed the concept of the series based on the idea of a treasure hunt.

David Levithan, executive editorial director at Scholastic, said Riordan was the company's first choice to write the initial book and provide direction for the series. Riordan appealed to Scholastic because he wrote for the ages, eight-to-twelve-year-olds, they want to reach; he had been a middle school teacher, and he was an avid gamer. Levithan liked the way Riordan combined action and adventure with humor and history. Scholastic had the general idea for the series, but asked Riordan to flesh out the cast of characters and then decide on the historical focus of each book. Riordan loved the challenge and idea of making world history fun for kids. It fit perfectly with his subversive learning philosophy. He found it exhilarating to take the team's concept and make it come to life.

Riordan kicked the series off in September 2008 with *The Maze of Bones*. Six other authors wrote the remaining nine books in the series, with a new book coming out every two or three months. *The Maze of Bones* is about orphans Amy and Dan Cahill, ages fourteen and eleven. When their wealthy grandmother Grace dies, she leaves a video with a challenge for her relatives, who she informs are members of one of the most important families in history. Fam-

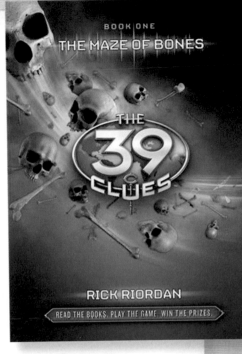

MAZE OF BONES

ily members could either accept 1 million dollars or the first of thirty-nine clues that would lead to a secret, if they could find it, that would make them the most powerful human beings on earth. Amy and Dan decide to accept the clue and pursue the secret that will take them around the world. Other family branches make the same decision, setting up an intense and dangerous race. *The Maze of Bones* reached number one on the *New York Times* best seller list on September 28, 2008.

First printing for *The Maze of Bones* was 500,000 copies and a multimillion-dollar advertising cam-paign was launched to support it. Scholastic, which had published the Harry Potter series, had a lot riding on the success of 39 Clues. Riordan provided name recognition and already had thousands of loyal followers. The popular author generated loads of media attention, appearing on the *Today Show* and giving interviews to the Associated Press, *USA Today*, *New York Times*, *Publisher's Weekly*, *Time*, and many others. It was big news when famed director Steven Spielberg and Dreamworks purchased the film rights to the 39 Clues series.

One of the series' goals was to appeal to kids who weren't regular readers. Ellie Berger, president

PEOPLE IN WORLD OF WARCRAFT COSTUMES AT DRAGONCON IN ATLANTA, GEORGIA, IN 2009

of Scholastic Trade, said the series would reach millions of kids worldwide—getting them excited about reading in a whole new way. Riordan, who admits to being a total geek when it comes to gaming, plays World of Warcraft online with his sons when he's traveling. He hoped the series would get kids who are interested in games and cards to read more. "Some kids may always prefer playing games to reading. But if I could convince even some of them that reading can be another way to have an adventure, I feel I have done my job," he says.

Riordan wrapped up the popular Percy Jackson series with the eagerly awaited *The Last Olympian,*

which had a first printing of 1.2 million copies and debuted at number one on *USA Today*'s best seller list. *The Last Olympian* is one of only a handful of children's books ever to debut at the top spot. In the series conclusion, Percy and his demigod friends must protect Mount Olympus from an army of titans and assorted monsters. Secret access to Mount Olympus is through the Empire State Building, and an epic battle unfolds in Manhattan. The stakes have never been higher as the fate of humanity and the gods hang in the balance.

*Booklist* wrote, "The novel's winning combination of high-voltage adventure and crackling wit is balanced with scenes in which human needs, fears and ethical choices take center stage . . . Riordan manages to bring the whole series to a satisfying close in the down-to-earth conclusion."

Riordan had originally envisioned the series as five books. Percy aged one year in each book, and Riordan

THE EMPIRE STATE BUILDING
IN MANHATTAN

didn't want to take him past age sixteen because he was most familiar with students from ages twelve to sixteen. Riordan confessed that it was difficult to end a series after having lived with a character for five years. At the same time, however, it was fun and gratifying to write a satisfying ending and bring together loose ends. He admitted it would have been easy to continue the series, but he had seen too many series go too long. When the author tires, the writing suffers and the books often become just slightly different versions of each other.

The conclusion of *The Last Olympian* revealed a new prophecy and hinted that more adventures were ahead. Riordan's legion of fans was left to wonder what exactly he had in mind.

# VII

# HOLLYWOOD AND
# TWO NEW SERIES

T he announcement that a movie was going to be made based on *The Lightning Thief* created a buzz among Percy Jackson fans. Riordan was peppered with questions about the movie at every book signing and appearance. The Riordans joked that Rick should get a button made that said, "Don't ask me about the movie" so he could wear it at all times. The most common questions readers asked were: "Are they really making a movie about the book?" "Can I be in the movie?" and "How much control do you have over the movie?"

CHRIS COLUMBUS AT THE PREMIERE OF *PERCY JACKSON
AND THE OLYMPIANS: THE LIGHTNING THIEF* IN
NEW YORK, ON FEBRUARY 4, 2010

Chris Columbus, director of the first two Harry Potter films, each of which grossed more than $300 million, was chosen to direct *The Lightning Thief*. Columbus also directed *Home Alone* and *Mrs. Doubtfire*. Author J. K. Rowling had insisted contractually that Columbus follow the Harry Potter books' storyline faithfully. Columbus earned praise for his directing efforts while adhering to the books' storyline. Famed director Steven Spielberg is said to have turned down the director's job because he didn't want to be obligated to follow the books.

With an excellent reputation in Hollywood, Columbus could be choosy about what films he directed. In 2007, his ten-year-old daughter, Isabella, who has ADHD, listened to an audio tape of *The Lightning Thief* and told her father he should read it. After he read the book, he was a big fan. It was different than anything he had ever read. He marveled at how the creatures and the stories of Greek mythology were all intertwined with modern society. He believed it was a cool idea for a movie.

He loved the book's message that something perceived as a weakness could not only be overcome, but actually turned into a strength. Columbus said kids with ADHD and dyslexia often feel they don't fit in. He wanted kids with disabilities to come away with the idea they aren't so different than Percy Jackson. Hopefully, they would be encouraged to turn the disability to their advantage and to feel like it may not be such a struggle. Columbus wanted the movie to be appreciated on two levels. He wanted kids ages seven to fifteen to thoroughly enjoy the action and the story line and for older kids and parents to feel like they were twelve years old again. He wanted the movie to be like a thrilling roller coaster ride. Columbus insisted, however, that he have complete directorial freedom that he lacked for the Harry Potter movies. He wanted to select the scenes and characters, control the pacing, and put his touch on the story.

Columbus knew comparisons to the Harry Potter films were inevitable, and he grew weary of answering questions on the topic. He acknowledged the similarities but stressed there were many more differences. Harry Potter and Percy Jackson live in two different worlds. Of course, Columbus was hoping to attract the same kind of audience as Harry Potter. After six movies, the Harry Potter films had accounted for $5 billion in box office revenue.

Prior to the opening of *The Lightning Thief*, a special screening was held for 450 kids. Their enthusiastic reaction boosted Columbus's confidence. He expected a significant word-of-mouth campaign since the targeted audience had grown up on cell phones, Twitter, and Facebook. The movie opened on February 12, 2010, with Logan Lerman starring as Percy Jackson, Alexandra Daddario as Annabeth, Brandon T. Jackson as Grover, Pierce Brosnan as Chiron, and Uma Thurman as Medusa. Surprisingly, Riordan chose not to see the movie, but his wife and children did. He said he would probably never see it because he has a strong image of what Percy and the other characters look like. He didn't want the movie images to replace his own. "I knew if I ever saw the movie I would never be able to get those images out of my head, and I didn't want that to happen," he said. Since he was still writing about Percy Jackson's world and the Heroes of Olympus series,

PIERCE BROSNAN (*LEFT*) AND BRANDON T. JACKSON IN A SCENE FROM THE MOVIE

he needed to keep his own vision clear. Riordan was annoyed when he read the seventh Harry Potter book and couldn't get the image of actor Daniel Radcliffe out of his mind. He wanted to be able to paint his own picture of Harry Potter, not accept the movie version. He likes the fact that his vision of Harry Potter or Percy Jackson might be different than others. Unfortunately, movies solidify the images, and when that happens, the story loses some of its magic for Riordan.

Riordan did read *The Lightning Thief* script and made some suggestions, but essentially he had no input into the movie. He was not, however, upset about his lack of input and involvement. He said selling one's book to Hollywood is akin to selling someone your house. "They can paint it a different color, tear it down and build something new, or do anything they want," he said.

*The Lightning Thief* opened to mixed reviews. Amy Biancolli of the *Houston Chronicle* wrote, "Director Chris Columbus has brought together the modern and mystical spheres with sharp pacing and a nifty sense of fun that atone for the film's dippier moments."

Rick Bentley of McClatchy Newspapers praised the film, "As the Harry Potter franchise has slipped deeper and deeper into dark areas, studios have been trying to find a film series that is imaginative and smart enough for young audiences. *The Lightning Thief* fulfills that quest . . . this is the start of something that could be really good."

The movie, however, fell short for some critics. Ethan Alter of Reuters wrote, "What's really lacking in *The Lightning Thief* is a genuine sense of wonder, the thing that brings viewers back to Hogwarts over and over. Percy's world seems like a decent place to visit, but it's not magical enough to make you want to live there."

*The Lightning Thief* was filmed in Vancouver, Canada, with an estimated budget of $95 million. It grossed $226 million worldwide, including $87 million in the United States. It was considered a modest success.

*The Lightning Thief* movie fueled sales of the Percy Jackson books as sales doubled. During the week of February 24, 2010, all five Percy Jackson books were on *USA Today*'s Top 10 list. It was the first time that had happened. Accounting for half of the Top 10 list was impressive, but Riordan didn't come close to Stephenie Meyer's feat of having all four titles from the Twilight series in the Top 10 for sixty-six weeks. J. K. Rowling had six of the seven Harry Potter books in the Top 10 for one week in 2007.

Alexandra Daddario, (LEFT), Logan Lerman, (CENTER), and Brandon
T. Jackson in one of the many action scenes from the movie

In 2010, Riordan launched two new series, The Kane Chronicles and Heroes of Olympus. Both were highly anticipated and debuted at number one on multiple best seller lists. When you have a series come out with a book a year, you build that anticipation and momentum, said Jonathan Yaged, U.S. publisher of the Disney Book Group. Topher Bradfield, children's outreach coordinator at BookPeople, added that the majority of kids prefer series. They want something that has a character who continues to grow, and they get comfortable following a character through a set of books and adventures.

The prolific author made the decision to have two series going at once, requiring him to write two books a year, instead of one. Although it was an incredible amount of pressure, Riordan was willing to juggle two writing projects and make the necessary sacrifices to keep his legion of fans happy. Riordan was excited about The Kane Chronicles because it was about Egyptian mythology, something new and fresh for him. He wanted to introduce the series, but he also didn't want to leave Percy Jackson fans waiting too long for the next chapter in the life of Percy and his friends.

Riordan admits he has a crazy writing schedule. "Nobody's making me do it," he said. "It's just a deadline I put on myself because I know kids can read faster than I can write and a year is about as long as

a kid wants to wait. A year when you're nine—that's an eternity." Why did Riordan select Egyptian mythology for The Kane Chronicles? One of the most frequent questions he was asked while doing appearances for the Percy Jackson books was, "Will you ever write about another mythology?" As a classroom teacher for fifteen years, Riordan knew that Ancient Egypt, which he enjoyed teaching, was the only subject close to his students' interest levels of the Greeks and Romans. Mummies, pyramids, hieroglyphics, curses, and strange animal-headed gods certainly appealed to middle school students. Egyptian mythology wasn't nearly as well known as Greek or Roman mythology. Riordan thought it was

AN EGYPTIAN COFFIN

an untapped subject in young adult literature, and that appealed to him. Like the Percy Jackson series, Riordan modernized the Egyptian myths by creating some young characters and a page-turning plot. He also mixed in his trademark humor and breathless action scenes.

*The Red Pyramid*, the first book in The Kane Chronicles, debuted in May 2010. It features siblings Carter and Sadie Kane, children of a mixed-race couple. Their mother was white and their father African American. Although brother and sister, the two don't really know each other. After their mother died, Sadie lived with her grandparents in London, and

Carter traveled around the world with his father, an Egyptologist. Carter and Sadie are brought together by their father in the British Museum. Using the Rosetta Stone to tap into a source of power, Dr. Kane opens a gateway that unleashes the gods into the modern world. In the process, Dr. Kane blows up the British Museum and is banished. The Kanes, descendants of Ancient Egyptian Magicians and Pharaohs, go on a world journey searching for their father and trying to save the world from destruction. The new series was an instant hit with young readers as *The Red Pyramid* sold 91,000 copies in the first week.

THE BRITISH MUSEUM
IN LONDON

In October 2010, *The Lost Hero*, the first book of the Heroes of Olympus was published. It had a first printing of 2.5 million books. *The Lost Hero* stars a new generation of demigods who train at Camp Half Blood. Riordan uses three narrators to tell the story: Jason, who wakes up on a school field trip bus without any memory of who he is or why he's there; Leo, a product of foster homes; and Piper, the daughter of a famous male movie star. The three join forces to pursue a challenging quest involving Hera, the queen of the gods.

*Throne of Fire*, the second book in The Kane Chronicles, was published in May 2011. Carter and Sadie have five days to save the world. They take turns telling the story in *Throne of Fire*. The duo once again battle Set, the god of evil, but their main concern is Apophis, the god of chaos, who is close to rising from the prison that has trapped him for centuries. The only way to stop him is to awaken Ra, the sun god, but no one knows where he is. They need to find the Book of Ra and learn to chant its spells in order to find and revive the Egyptian god.

With his intense writing schedule, soaring popularity, and increased demands on his time, Riordan had to make the difficult decision to cut back on his school visits and book signings. In the early days of Percy Jackson, Riordan was able to take time to talk with each child, personalize the autograph, and even have his photo taken with the child. That was no longer possible. For example, a book signing in Denver in October 2011 attracted five hundred people. Riordan told the crowd that ten people showed up the first time he visited the bookstore after the publication of *The Lightning Thief.* Additionally, he could no longer reply to the overwhelming volume of personal e-mails and letters. While that's disappointing to his fans, Riordan believes his time is better spent writing so his fans don't have to wait so long for the next book. He communicates with his fans via his blog, which he has maintained since 2005. With the days of writing in relative obscurity in the past, Riordan was now learning how to handle a magnitude of fame that few writers ever experience.

# A Rock Star, of Sorts

The town of Columbia, South Carolina, had never seen anything like it. An estimated crowd of 3,000 people, mostly excited youngsters with their parents, lined up along the street, six-to-eight deep for more than a mile outside the Books-A-Million store. Many youngsters had dressed as their favorite god or character. The crowd waited patiently for the arrival of author Rick Riordan. When he finally came into view, he was riding in a horse-drawn carriage, the same way the god Hades would have traveled. The crowd enthusiastically cheered and applauded. The Books-A-Million staff had used a Hades theme to decorate the store to host a book signing by Riordan, who spent several hours autographing copies of his books.

Jacquie Lee, Books-A-Million's regional community relations manager, said, "It was as though Riordan was a rock star. I've been in this business close to 30 years, and have even hosted U.S. presidents, but this was perhaps the most intense event I've witnessed. To see the look on those children's faces was amazing."

Columbia was the first stop in an Olympian Week tour across the country in October 2011 to celebrate the release of *Son of Neptune*, the second book in the Heroes of Olympus series. *Son of Neptune* had an unprecedented first printing of 3 million copies, the most in Disney Publishing Worldwide history. It shot to the top of the major national best seller lists. During the seven-day, seven-city tour, winners of a contest that Disney-Hyperion held for U.S. and Canadian bookstores and libraries hosted Riordan. Each winner selected a different god as a theme for their decorations and activities.

Pittsburgh was the second stop, and a sold-out crowd of six hundred people at the Carnegie Public Library greeted Riordan. After delivering a brief talk, Riordan took questions from a panel of four students dressed in costumes and the general audience. He then signed copies of his book. When one boy, wearing a tuxedo, approached Riordan with a book to autograph, Riordan asked him about his unusual apparel. "I wore it to meet you," he said. "This is the best night of my life."

In Toronto, more than 1,000 screaming fans welcomed him at a Chapters Bookstore. It was as if Justin Bieber, Selena Gomez, or Taylor Swift had arrived. The following day, more than 2,500 people attended the event at the Barnes & Noble in Burlington, Massachusetts. Fans, some coming from as far away as New Jersey and New York, started to line up outside the store in the early morning for the evening program.

In Mission Viejo, California, Riordan arrived at the Mission Viejo Library in a chariot pulled by Spartan warriors. A crowd of 3,500 fans lined the street and cheered his arrival. Alexander Uhl, owner of A Whale of a Tale Children's Bookshoppe, rode with Riordan in the chariot. It was an unreal experience. Uhl said, "Riding with Rick Riordan to thunderous applause and the roar of the crowd was like scoring the winning touchdown in the Super Bowl." The tour ended with Riordan arriving by yacht at the Port of Olympia Plaza in Olympia, Washington, as 3,500 fans gave him a warm, energetic welcome. The plaza was turned into "Poseidon's Fish Market" as twenty-five tents featured seaside-themed crafts and activities. During the week-long tour, Riordan signed more than 25,000 books.

Despite his success, Riordan has changed little other than leaving his full-time job at Saint Mary's Hall. Up until 2009, he lived in the same home he

RICK RIORDAN SPEAKS AT THE BOOK LAUNCH CELEBRATION FOR
*THE LOST HERO* IN OCTOBER 2010 IN AUSTIN, TEXAS.

had before the success of the Percy Jackson books. That year, the Riordan family moved to a slightly larger home in the same San Antonio neighborhood, just two miles away. The home has a swimming pool and a private study for Riordan to write. He prefers driving a minivan rather than a sports car. And, he would rather spend time with his wife and two sons than with the rich and famous.

When asked why he hasn't chosen a wealthier lifestyle, he replied, "We like to keep things simple. I didn't become a full-time writer until I was almost 40. So my identity was really shaped before that." Riordan tries to minimize the impact of fame and success on his family. His first job is being a dad and being with his family. Writing comes second.

After interviewing Riordan for a feature on NBC's *Rock Center* in 2012, correspondent Kate Snow said, "Rick is just about the most humble author I've ever met." Riordan says he's been blessed to have a lot of very grounded people, particularly his wife of twenty-six years, around him. "She would not tolerate me getting a big head," he says. He calls his wife, Becky, a saint and adds that she is the most good-natured, even keeled, practical, and wonderful person he has ever met. Becky handles much of the business side of Rick's successful career, allowing him more time to write.

Riordan's popularity was never more evident than in 2011. He had six books on *USA Today*'s Top 100 Books for 2011: number fourteen: *Son of Neptune*; number twenty-five: *Throne of Fire*; number forty-three: *The Lost Hero*; number sixty-nine: *The Red Pyramid*; number eighty: *The Lightning Thief*; and number eighty-seven: *The Last Olympian*. The national list included books of all genres, not just young adult books. The hardcover version of *The Red Pyramid* enjoyed a sixty-five week run on the *New York Times* best seller list for children's chapter books.

When *Forbes* released its list of the highest-paid authors for 2011, Riordan was sixth on the list, having made $21 million. Stephenie Meyer also earned the same amount. Riordan was ahead of well-known authors such as Dean Koontz ($19 million), John Grisham ($18 million), Jeff Kinney ($17 million), and Nicholas Sparks ($16 million). Only four authors made more: James Patterson ($84 million), Danielle Steele ($35 million),

STEPHENIE MEYER

Stephen King ($28 million), and Janet Evanovich ($22 million).

In January 2012, an exhibit featuring the life and works of Rick Riordan opened at Texas State University's Wittliff Collections in San Marcos, Texas. Riordan had generously donated numerous artifacts to the museum since 2004. The exhibit gave visitors an understanding of Riordan's work process, how his life as a middle school teacher prepared him to write for children, and how he can take real-life episodes and turn them into literary scenes and stories, according to curator Steve Davis. The first manuscript Riordan submitted at age thirteen and the accompanying rejection letter, the original *The Lightning Thief* manuscript, his hand-drawn map of Camp Half Blood, marketing materials for his books, a sample of the thousands of letters he receives annually from fans, and the actual sword, "Riptide," used in the film version of *The Lightning Thief* were all displayed.

In 2012, Riordan was named Author of the Year for *The Lost Hero* in the Children's Book Award voting. Since the votes of more than 524,000 children determined the award, it was especially meaningful to Riordan, who values children's literary opinions. *The Red Pyramid* also was named the fifth and sixth grade book of the year. The award caught Riordan completely off guard. Although he

SUZANNE COLLINS

attended the awards announcement in New York City, he didn't prepare any remarks in case he won. He hadn't figured on beating out an impressive field that included authors Jeff Kinney, Suzanne Collins, and Stephenie Meyer.

*The Serpent's Shadow*, the final book in The Kane Chronicles, debuted in May 2012 with a first printing of 2 million copies. Carter and Sadie must destroy Apophis, who threatens to plunge the world into eternal darkness, once and for all. But it won't be easy.

The Heroes of Olympus series concluded with *Mark of Athena* in 2012. Percy, Hazel, and Frank who met at Camp Jupiter in *Son of Neptune* team up with Jason, Piper, and Leo from *The Lost Hero* to defeat the giants released by the Earth Monster, Gaea. But who is the seventh person referred to in the prophecy?

Rick Riordan's books have sold more than 30 million copies and been translated into thirty-seven languages. When people asked Riordan if Percy Jackson was the next Harry Potter, he replied that there is only one Harry Potter and there will never be another. The success of Harry Potter was completely unprecedented in young adult literature. J. K. Rowling's books have sold a whopping 450 million copies worldwide. Riordan doesn't believe that feat will ever be duplicated. While he's flattered that he is often compared to J. K. Rowling and Percy Jackson is often mentioned as the next Harry Potter, he says his main goal is to just keep entertaining readers. And while other writers may measure their success in book sales, he measures his by anecdotes—the kid who said he never liked to read before reading *The Lightning Thief*; the parent who thanked him for turning her daughter onto reading; or the teacher who said he helped turn her class around because they bonded over reading Percy Jackson every day.

After writing eight adult mysteries, five Percy Jackson books, three The Kane Chronicles books, three Heroes of Olympus books and one The 39 Clues book, Riordan shows no signs of slowing down. When Riordan was asked if it was difficult for him to come up with ideas, he said it was just the opposite. He has so many ideas it is hard to narrow them down.

That's good news for all of his loyal readers. His next series will feature Norse mythology. In 2011, he announced he had signed a deal with Disney Publishing Worldwide, his current publisher, for at least three books. Riordan is excited about the series because there are so many fantastic stories to tell. He wants to bring Thor and Odin and Norse mythology into the modern world just as he did Percy Jackson and Greek mythology. His fans will probably have to wait until 2015 for the series to debut.

Before that, however, Percy Jackson fans will be able to view *Sea of Monsters* in theaters. Twentieth Century Fox announced the entire cast from *The Lightning Thief*, including Logan Lerman as Percy, will return for the sequel, which is due in theaters March 2013. The film is expected to spur sales of the Percy Jackson books and bring new fans to the series.

Despite all of his success, Riordan doesn't take any of it for granted. In 2011, Riordan and his wife, Becky, attended a Lyle Lovett concert at the Majestic Theater in San Antonio. Lovett, a country singer from Texas, is one of Rick's favorite performers. During his concert, Lovett said he wanted to be a musician when he was growing up in Houston. But making stuff up wasn't a real job where he came from. But thanks to all of his fans, it became one. Riordan can relate to that. "I'm grateful to have made a career telling stories—and it's thanks to my readers," he says.

BRANDON T. JACKSON, (*LEFT*), LOGAN LERMAN, (*CENTER*), AND ALEXANDRA DADDARIO IN *THE LIGHTNING THIEF*

# TIMELINE

1964   Born on June 5 in San Antonio, Texas.

1977   Submits short story to *Isaac Asimov's Science Fiction* magazine; story rejected.

1982   Graduates from Alamo Heights High School in San Antonio.

1982   Enrolls at North Texas State in Denton.

1984   Transfers to University of Texas at Austin.

1986   Graduates from the University of Texas at Austin.

1986   Marries Becky, his high school sweetheart.

1987   Takes first teaching position at New Breunfels Middle School in San Antonio.

1990   Accepts a teaching position with Presidio Hill School and moves to San Francisco.

1997   Publishes first novel *Big Red Tequila*.

1988   Moves back to San Antonio and accepts a teaching position with Saint Mary's Hall School.

2002   Honored with Master Teacher Award from Saint Mary's Hall School.

| 2003 | Inducted into the Texas Institute of Letters. |
| 2005 | Quits teaching after receiving an advance for *The Lightning Thief.* |
| 2005 | Publishes *The Lightning Thief.* |
| 2007 | *The Lightning Thief* makes the *New York Times* best seller list. |
| 2010 | *The Lightning Thief* movie opens. |
| 2011 | *Son of Neptune* has a first printing of 3 million copies; has six books on *USA Today's* Top 100 for the year. |
| 2011 | Ranks sixth on *Forbes*'s list of highest paid authors for the year; made $21 million. |

# SOURCES

CHAPTER 1  CREATIVE INFLUENCES

p. 13,  "Rick, this is great . . ." "Proud Products of Texas Public Schools: Rick Riordan," Texas Association of School Boards, https://www.tasb.org/about/schools/proud_products/rick_riordan.aspx.

p. 13,  "angels aren't science fiction . . ." Michael Cox, "Riordan's Rules for Writing," *Courier*, October 18, 2008.

p. 16,  "Well, bring it along . . ."*Myth and Mystery*; "A Father's Day Past," in *Myth and Mystery*, a blog by Rick Riordan, June 18, 2011, http://rickriordan.blogspot.com.

p. 18,  "The foundation of who . . ." Ibid.

p. 19,  "I'm convinced this . . ." *Myth and Mystery*; "Flying on Mother's Day," in *Myth and Mystery*; a blog by Rick Riordan, May 13, 2007, http://rickriordan.blogspot.com.

p. 19,  "That boxed set . . ." Jane Sullivan, "Unwrapping the Gift of Childhood Rapture," *Brisbane Times*, December 16, 2011, http://www.brisbanetimes.com.au/society-and-culture/unwrapping-the-gift-of-rapture-20111216-loylw.html.

p. 20,  "a tale of enthralling . . ." "' The Lord of the Rings' Book," http://www.lord-of-the-rings.org/books.html.

p. 21,  "Those times I spent . . ." Rick Riordan, interview with Lori Polydoros, Society of Children's Books Writers & Illustrators, December 2007, http://www.scbwi.org/Pages.aspx/Rick-Riordan.

p. 21,  "Write what you know," Rick Riordan, interview with Lyn Belisle, mother of Rick Riordan, http://www.trinity.edu/org/tricksters/trixway/current/vol%205/part1/Lyn_Belisle.pdf.

CHAPTER 2  GETTING PUBLISHED

p. 30,  "It was only after moving . . ." Rick Riordan, interview with Graham Marks, http://www.justimaginestorycentre.co.uk.

p. 33,  "It felt different . . ." Judyth Rigler, "S.A. Roots Run Deep for Writer," *San Antonio Express-News*, July 13, 1997.

p. 33,  "I knew, deep down . . ." *Myth and Mystery*; "Why Write Novels?," in *Myth and Mystery*; a blog by Rick Riordan, September 9, 2006, http://rickriordan.blogspot.com.

p. 34,  "We love the story . . ." Alison Follos, "Author Profile: Rick Riordan," *Library Media Connection*, 103, no. 5 (February 4, 2008).

p. 34,  "A stand out . . ." Unsigned review of *Big Red Tequilla* by *Publishers Weekly*.

p. 34,  "Texas ambience served . . ." Unsigned review of *Big Red Tequilla*, by *Portland Oregonian*.

p. 34,  "Riordan writes so well . . ." Unsigned review of *Big Red Tequilla*, by *Chicago Tribune*.

p. 34,  "Riordan's sense of place . . ." Sterlin Holmesly, "'Big Red Tequila' Heady Draft: Strong Sense of Place Enlivens S. A. Expatriates First Novel," *San Antonio Express-News*, July 13, 1997.

## CHAPTER 3 Percy Jackson is Born

p. 37, "Today, I'm constantly . . ." *Myth and Mystery*; "My Overnight Success," in *Myth and Mystery*; a blog by Rick Riordan, December 22, 2007, http://rickriordan.blogspot.com.

p. 40, "Riordan shows measurable . . ." Sterlin Holmesly, "Texas Two-Step A Snappy Trot," *San Antonio Express-News*, July 5, 1998.

pp. 42-43, "It's appropriate that . . ." Oline H. Cogdill, "Sleuth's Trest: Find Prof's Killer," *Sun-Sentinel*, March 19, 2000.

p. 46, "I should probably . . ." Bridget Gutierrez, "Master Teachers: Four at St. Mary's Hall Get $10,000 Prizes for Excellence," *San Antonio Express-News*, October 22, 2002.

p. 47, "Why can't you just . . ." Sally Williams, "Percy Jackson: My Boy's Own Adventure," *Guardian* (UK), February 5, 2010, http://www.guardian.co.uk/lifeandstyle2010/feb/08/percy-jackson-rick-riordan.

p. 47, "No one will be . . ." Sharyn Vane, "Percy Jackson's Creator Talks About Creating the Bestselling Series and Bringing it to a Close, *Austin American-Statesman*, May 3, 2009, http://statesman.com/life/content/life/stories/books/05/03/0503kidsbooks.html.

## CHAPTER 4 *The Lighning Thief*

p. 50, "Kids are a tougher . . ." Jeannette Larson, "Talking With Rick Riordan," American Library Association, http://www.ala.org/ala/aboutala/offices/publishing/booklinks/resources/riordan.cfm.

p. 51, "This is a whole different . . ." Steve Bennett, "A Happy Ending—San Antonio Writer Turns a Bedtime Tale Into a Children's Book Series," *San Antonio News-Express*, August 29, 2004.

p. 52, "It's a book that combines an ordinary . . ." Ibid.

p. 53, "I want to inspire . . ." Lauren Barack, "Rick Riordan on His Latest Mega Sellter 'The Red Pyramid,'" *School Library Journal*, July 1, 2010, http://www.libraryjournal.com/slj/articlescertification/885597-342/rick_riordan_on_his-latest.html.csp.

p. 54, "That's it. Nobody . . ." *Myth and Mystery*; "My Overnight Success," in *Myth and Mystery*; a blog by Rick Riordan.

p. 55, "We have a desire . . ." Chauncey Mabe, "Rick Riordan: Percy Jackson vs. Harry Potter," May 14, 2009, http://weblogs.sun-sentinel.com.

p. 55, "There's so much to spark . . ." Ibid.

p. 56, "It's the same idea . . ." *Myth and Mystery*; "The Stolen Chariot, Part Two," in *Myth and Mystery*; a blog by Rick Riordan, July 25, 2007, http://rickriordan.blogspot.com.

p. 56, "about being irreverent . . ." Steve Bennett, "S. A. Writer Has a Monstrous Side—No, Really," *San Antonio News-Express*, May 4, 2008.

p. 57, "They're stuck in . . ." Ibid.

pp. 57-58, *"The Lightning Thief* is perfectly . . ."* Polly Shulman, "Harry Who?" *New York Times*, November 13, 2005, http://www.nytimes.com/2005/11/13/books/review/13shulman.html?pagewanted=print.

p. 58, "He's the teacher you never . . ." Steve Bennett, "Author Spends Time in Two Worlds," *San Antonio Express-News*, July 8, 2005.

## CHAPTER 5 A LEGION OF FANS GROWS

p. 62, "Riordan crafts a sequel . . ." Unsigned review by *Publishers Weekly*.

p. 65, "Dyslexia . . . is simply . . ." Sharyn Wizda Vane, "Talking With Rick Riordan," *Austin American-Statesman*, May 3, 2009, http://www.statesman.com.

p. 65, "I used to feel like dyslexia," Chloe Lambert, " Ritalin Tore My Son and Our Family Apart," *Daily Mail*, February 1, 2011, http://www.dailymail.co.uk/health/article- http://www.dailymail.co.uk/health/article-1352338/Ritalin-How-ADHD-drug-tore-best-selling-children-authors-family-apart.html.

p. 66, "You can do so much . . ." Laura Lea, "Best-selling Author Helping Son Share His Story," December 14, 2011, http://www.woai.com/news/local/story/Best-selling-author-helping-son-share-his-story/ljl.

p. 66 "You don't have to have . . ." Christina Kristofic, "Author Strikes at Students' Hearts," *Intelligencer*, April 29, 2009.

pp. 66-67, "No—I got it from Hercules . . ." Melissa Wiley, "SDCC 2010: The Rick Riordan Panel," July 28, 2010, http://melissawiley.com/blog/2010/07/28/sdcc-2010-the-rick-riordan-panel.

p. 67, "I've just described . . ." Williams, "Percy Jackson: My Boy's Own Adventure."

p. 68, "Because there's nothing . . ." Ibid.

## CHAPTER 6 MYTHS, MYSTERY, AND A UNIQUE SERIES

p. 74, "High-powered action sequences . . ." Unsigned review by *Kirkus* www.barnesandnoble.com.

p. 77, "No book has ever . . ." *Myth and Mystery*; "Top Five Misconceptions about Writing: A Keynote Address from '06," in *Myth and Mystery*; a blog by Rick Riordan, January 26, 2011, http://rickriordan.blogspot.com.

p. 83, "Some kids may always . . ." Ibid.; "The 39 Reactions," in *Myth and Mystery*; a blog by Rick Riordan, December 24, 2007, http://rickriordan.blogspot.com.

p. 84, "The novel's winning . . ." Unsigned review by *Booklist*.

CHAPTER 7 HOLLYWOOD AND TWO NEW SERIES

p. 90,     "I knew if I ever . . ." Dave Banks, "Greek Goddesses and Roman Gods:
           The Geekdad Interview with Rick Riordan," October 18, 2010, Wired.
           com, http://www.wired.com/geekdad/2010/10/rick-riordan-interview/.
           www.wired.com/geekdad.

p. 92,     "They can paint it . . ." Rick Riordan, interview with Lood, October 11,
           2011, http://blog.exclus1ves.co.za/an-interview-with-rick-riordan.

p. 92,     "Director Chris Columbus . . ." Connie Ann Kirk, "'Percy Jackson'
           Reviews—What Do the Critics Think?," February 16, 2010, Examiner.com,
           http://www.Examiner.com/article/percy-jackson-reviews-what-do-the-
           critics-think.

pp. 92-93, "As the Harry Potter franchise . . ." Steve Bennett, "The Lightning Thief Is
           Not a Potter Rip-Off," San Antonio Express-News, February 12, 2010.

p. 93,     "What's really lacking . . ." Connie Ann Kirk, "Chris Columbus compares
           directing 'Harrp Potter' and 'Percy Jackson,'" February 11, 2010,
           Examiner.com, http://www.examiner.com/article/chris-columbus-
           compares-directing-harry-potter-and-percy-jackson.

pp. 96-97, "Nobody's making me . . ." Banks, "Greek Goddesses and Roman Gods:
           The Geekdad Interview with Rick Riordan."

CHAPTER 8 A ROCK STAR, OF SORTS

p. 104,    "It was as though . . ." Sally Lodge, "Rick Riordan Wraps Up Whirlwind
           Olympian Week Tour," Publishers Weekly, October 20, 2011, http://www.
           publishersweekly.com/pw/by-topic/childrens/childrens book news/
           article/491.

p. 104,    "I wore it to meet you . . ." Ibid.

p. 105,    "Riding with Rick Riordan . . ." Ibid.

p. 108,    "We like to keep . . ." Karen MacPherson, "Corner: Rick Riordan's 'Red
           Pyramid' Conjures Up Ancient Egypt," Scripps Howard News Service,
           May 3, 2010.

p. 108,    "Rick is just about the most humble . . ." Kate Snow, "Changing the Way
           Kids Look at the World, One Book at a Time," NBC Rock Center, January
           9, 2012.

p. 108,    "She would not tolerate . . ." Ibid.

p. 113,    "I'm grateful . . ." Myth and Mystery; "Music, Mullets, and A Journey of
           Three Decades," in Myth and Mystery; a blog by Rick Riordan, July 3,
           2011, http://rickriordan.blogspot.com.

# BIBLIOGRAPHY

Banks, Dave. "Greek Goddesses and Roman Gods: The GeekDad Interview with Rick Riordan." October 18, 2010. http://www.wired.com/geekdad/2010/10/rick-riordan-interview.

Barack, Lauren. "Rick Riordan on His Latest Mega Seller 'The Red Pyramid.'" *Library Journal*, July 1, 2010. http://www.libraryjournal.com/slj/articlescertification/885597-342/rick_riordan_on_his-latest.html.csp.

Bennett, Steve. "A Happy Ending: San Antonio Writer Turns a Bedtime Tale into a Children's Book Series." *San Antonio Express-News*, August 29, 2004. http://infoweb.newsbank.com/iw-search/we/InfoWeb.

———. "S.A. Writer Has a Monstrous Side—No, Really." *San Antonio Express-News*, May 4, 2008. http://infoweb.newsbank.com/iw-search/we/InfoWeb.

———. "Author Spends Time in Two Worlds." *San Antonio Express-News*, July 8, 2005. http://infoweb.newsbank.com/iw-search/we/InfoWeb.

———. "The Lightning Thief Is Not a Potter Rip-off." *San Antonio Express-News*, February 12, 2010. http://infoweb.newsbank.com/iw-search/we/InfoWeb.

Cogdill, Oline. "Sleuth's Test: Find Prof's Killer." *Sun-Sentinel*, March 19, 2000. http://infoweb.newsbank.com/iw-search/we/InfoWeb.

Cox, Michael. "Riordan's Rules for Writing." *Courier*, October 18, 2008. http://infoweb.newsbank.com/iw-search/we/InfoWeb.

Follos, Alison. "Rejection is a Powerful Thing." Library Media Connection, August 20, 2003. http://encore.yorklibraries.org:50080/wilson-base/hww/results.

Gutierrez, Bridget. "Four at St. Mary's Hall Get $10,000 Prizes for Excellence." *San Antonio Express News,* October 22, 2002. http://infoweb.newsbank.com/iw-searche/we/InfoWeb.

Holmesly, Sterlin. "Texas Two-Step is a Snappy Trot." *San Antonio Express-News*, July 5, 1998. http://infoweb.newsbank.com/iw-search/we/InfoWeb.

Kirk, Connie Ann. "Percy Jackson Reviews: What Do the Critics Think?" *Entertainment Examiner*, February 16, 2010. http://infoweb.newsbank.com/iw-search/we/InfoWeb.

———. "Chris Columbus Compares Directing Harry Potter and Percy Jackson." *Entertainment Examiner*, February 11, 2010. http://infoweb.newsbank.com/iw-search/we/InfoWeb.

Kristofic, Christina. "Author Strikes at Students' Hearts." *Intelligencer*, April 29, 2009. http://infoweb.newsbank.com/iw-search/we/InfoWeb.

Lambert, Chloe. "Ritalin Tore My Son and Our Family Apart." *Daily Mail*, February 1, 2011. http://www.dailymail.co.uk/health/article-1352338/Ritalin-How-ADHD-drug-tore-best-selling-children-authors-family-apart.html.

Larson, Jeanette. "Talking with Rick Riordan." http://www.ala.org/ala/aboutala/offices/publishing/booklinks/resources/riordan.cfm.

Lea, Laura. "Best-selling Author Helping Son Share His Story." December 15, 2011. http://www.woai.com/news/local/story/Best-selling-author-helping-son-share-his-story/ljl.

Lodge, Sally. "Rick Riordan Wraps Up Whirlwind Olympian Week Tour." *Publishers Weekly*, October 20, 2011. http://www.publishersweekly.com/pw/by-topic/childrens/childrens-book-news/article/491.

Mabe, Chauncey. "Rick Riordan: Percy Jackson vs. Harry Potter." May 14, 2009. www.weblogs.sun-sentinel.com/features/arts/offthepage/blog/2009/05/rick_riordan_percy-jackson_vs_1.html.

MacPherson, Karen. "Rick Riordan's Red Pyramid Conjures up Ancient Egypt." Scripps Howard News Service, May 3, 2010.

Polydoros, Lori. "Interview with Rick Riordan." December 2007. http://www.scbwi.org/Pages.aspx/Rick-Riordan.

Rigler, Judyth. "S.A. Roots Run Deep for Writer." *San Antonio Express-News*, July 13, 1997. http://infoweb.newsbank.com/iw-search/we/InfoWeb.

Riordan, Rick. "Music, Mullets and a Journey of Three Decades." June 27, 2011. http://rickriordan.blogspot.com

———. "Why Write Novels?" September 9, 2006. http://rickriordan. blogspot.com.

———. "My Overnight Success." December 22, 2007. http:// rickriordan.blogspot.com.

———. "Flying on Mother's Day." May 13, 2007. http://rickriordan. blogspot.com.

———. "The Frontiers of Mythology." July 25, 2007. http://rickriordan. blogspot.com.

———. "The 39 Reactions." December 24, 2007. http://rickriordan. blogspot.com.

———. "A Father's Day Past." June 18, 2011.http://rickriordan. blogspot.com.

Shulman, Polly. "Harry Who?" *New York Times*, November 13, 2005. http://www.nytimes.com/2005/11/13/books/review/13shulman. html?pagewanted=print.

Snow, Kate. "Changing the Way Kids Look at the World, One Book at a Time." January 9, 2012. www.nbcnews.com.

Sullivan, Jane. "Unwrapping the Gift of Childhood Rapture." December 16, 2011. http://www.brisbanetimes.com.au/society-and-culture/unwrapping-the-gift-of-rapture-20111216-loylw.html.

Vane, Sharyn. "Percy Jackson's Creator Talks about Creating the Bestselling Series and Bringing It to a Close." May 3, 2009. http:// statesman.com/life/content/life/stories/books/05/03/0503kidsbooks. html.

Williams, Sally. "Percy Jackson: My Boy's Own Adventure." *The Guardian*, February 5, 2010. http://www.guardian.co.uk/ lifeandstyle2010/feb/08/percy-jackson-rick-riordan.

# WEB SITES

http://www.rickriordan.com
RIORDAN'S OFFICIAL ONLINE SITE.

http://rickriordan.blogspot.com.
*MYTH AND MYSTERY,* THE OFFICIAL BLOG FOR THE AUTHOR.

# INDEX

# PHOTO CREDITS